Romeo and Juliet
25 Key Quotations for GCSE

Mark Birch

Series Editor: Hannah Rabey

firestonebooks.com

Romeo and Juliet
25 Key Quotations for GCSE
Mark Birch

Series Editor: Hannah Rabey

2021 Edition

ISBN-13: 978-1909608306

Published by Firestone Books

firestonebooks.com

You can stay up to date by following Firestone Books on Facebook and Twitter, or subscribing to our fabulous newsletter. Go on – you know you want to…

Contents

About this Book

The GCSE English Literature exam relies on understanding a wide range of relevant references, studied both in lessons and as part of revision. This guide will provide you with in-depth analysis of 25 key quotations in William Shakespeare's play *Romeo and Juliet*, written by experts to ensure that you are prepared for success.

In this guide you will find:

- A chronology of the quotations throughout the play
- A biography of William Shakespeare's life
- A summary of the key events in each act of the play
- 25 key analysed quotations
- A key terms glossary

The 25 quotations include:

- Detailed analysis of the quotation
- Key context relating to the quotation
- A list of key themes and characters that the quotation links to (key terms are denoted by an asterisk)

A Chronology of the Quotations in this Guide

Act One

Quotation 1: Prologue: 'A pair of star-crossed lovers take their life'

Quotation 2: Scene 1: 'My naked weapon is out. Quarrel, I will back thee.'

Quotation 3: Scene 1: '...peace? I hate the word, / As I hate hell, all Montagues and thee.'

Quotation 4: Scene 1: 'O brawling love, O loving hate... / O heavy lightness... / Feather of lead, bright smoke, cold fire, sick health!'

Quotation 5: Scene 2: 'She's the hopeful lady of my earth'

Quotation 6: Scene 4: 'Some consequence yet hanging in the stars.'

Quotation 7: Scene 5: '...she hangs upon the cheek of night / As a rich jewel in an Ethiop's ear.'

Quotation 8: Scene 5: 'If I profane with my unworthiest hand / This holy shrine, the gentle sin is this, / My lips, two blushing pilgrims, ready stand.'

Quotation 9: Scene 5: 'My only love sprung from my only hate!'

Act Two

Quotation 10: Scene 2: 'It is the east, and Juliet is the sun. / Arise, fair sun, and kill the envious moon...'

Quotation 11: Scene 2: 'O Romeo, Romeo, wherefore art thou Romeo? / Deny thy father and refuse thy name...'

Quotation 12: Scene 2: 'That which we call a rose / By any other name would smell as sweet'

Quotation 13: Scene 2: 'It is too rash, too unadvis'd, too sudden, / Too like the lightning'

Quotation 14: Scene 3: 'Wisely and slow; they stumble that run fast.'

Quotation 15: Scene 6: 'These violent delights have violent ends, / And in their triumph die like fire and powder.'

Act Three

Quotation 16: Scene 1: 'A plague o'both your houses!'

Quotation 17: Scene 1: 'Ask for me tomorrow, and you shall find me a grave man'

Quotation 18: Scene 2: '...when I shall die, / Take him and cut him out in little stars'

Quotation 19: Scene 2: 'Beautiful tyrant, fiend angelical! / Dove-feather'd raven, wolvish-ravening lamb!'

Quotation 20: Scene 3: 'In what vile part of this anatomy / Doth my name lodge? Tell me, that I may sack / The hateful mansion.'

Quotation 21: Scene 5: 'Out, you green-sickness carrion! Out, you baggage! / You tallow-face!'

Quotation 22: Scene 5: 'Romeo's a dishclout to him. An eagle, madam, / Hath not so green, so quick, so fair an eye / As Paris hath.'

Act Five

Quotation 23: Scene 1: 'Then I defy you, stars!'

Quotation 24: Scene 3: 'Thou detestable maw, thou womb of death, / Gorg'd with the dearest morsel of the earth.'

Quotation 25: Scene 3: '...shake the yoke of inauspicious stars / From this world-wearied flesh.'

A Biography of William Shakespeare

Born in Stratford-upon-Avon in 1564, William Shakespeare is arguably the greatest writer in English Literature. His father was a wealthy businessman and Shakespeare was probably educated in the town's Grammar School. He married Anne Hathaway at the age of eighteen and had three children, although his son, Hamnet, died in 1586.

At some point in the next ten years, Shakespeare moved to London and joined the company of actors known as *The Lord Chamberlain's Men* and began to write for the company. In 1603, the company received royal patronage and became *The King's Men*, performing some plays to King James at the royal court.

Shakespeare's works were highly successful and, unusually, he received a share in the takings from the theatres in which the company worked. Dedicated buildings for the performance of plays were a recent addition to London, built beyond the jurisdiction of the city in order to avoid the licensing of performance spaces introduced in 1574. Most plays had previously been performed in the courtyards of inns and the first theatres were built around the structure of these courtyards, being circular or hexagonal, with balconies around the walls. *The Globe*, built in 1599, where Shakespeare's company staged most of its plays, utilised the same timber used in the construction of England's first dedicated space for the performance of plays: Burbage's *The Theatre,* built in 1576.

Artificial light and sets were not used in early theatres and performances took place during the day, requiring playwrights to indicate time and setting through the language of the play or aspects of staging. In *Romeo and Juliet*, night is sometimes indicated through the use of torchbearers. Shakespeare allows the audience to recognise that Act Two, Scene Three of the play takes place at dawn because Friar Lawrence's first words are, 'The grey-eyed morn smiles on the frowning night...' It was unlawful for women to perform on the stage, so all female roles were played by boys, an accepted convention by the time Shakespeare staged *Romeo and Juliet*.

The narrative of *Romeo and Juliet* was a familiar one to Shakespeare's contemporaries. The basic story appeared in the Italian short stories of Bandello and Salernitano, but it was also found in other prose and dramatic works by the mid-sixteenth century. Shakespeare was probably familiar with it through Arthur Brooke's narrative poem *The Tragicall History of Romeus and Juliet*, written in 1562. While Shakespeare largely follows the narrative of Brooke's work, the differences between the poem and Shakespeare's play are noteworthy. The narrative of the poem takes place over nine months, while Shakespeare condenses this to just five days; Juliet's age is reduced to 13 and characters such as the Nurse and Mercutio are significantly developed. Perhaps the most striking difference is that Brooke condemns the actions of his characters while Shakespeare represents the young lovers more sympathetically.

Romeo and Juliet is likely to have been produced in the first phase of Shakespeare's dramatic works, probably between 1594 and 1596 but there has been considerable critical debate regarding the dating of the plays. The first quarto (a small book where the pages are folded for economy) version of the play appeared in 1597, entitled 'An excellent conceited tragedie of Romeo and Juliet'. This unauthorised printing was probably based on a text constructed from the recollections of those who knew the play from the stage. A second quarto was published in 1599, 'Newly corrected, augmented and amended'. The quartos had no division by Act or Scene, with these only appearing in the First Folio* edition of 1623, which contained 36 of Shakespeare's plays. *Romeo and Juliet* appeared in the tragedy section.

While Shakespeare appears to have devoted most of his creativity to the production of plays, he published two narrative poems in 1593-4, perhaps as a result of the closure of all theatres following an outbreak of the plague. Shakespeare was a prolific poet and a quarto of his sonnets* was published in 1609; this quarto contained over 150 sonnets, probably written during the 1590s. The meter* of the sonnets, iambic* pentameter*, also dominates Shakespeare's plays and he introduces Acts One and Two of *Romeo and Juliet* with sonnets delivered by the Chorus*. The first verbal exchange between Romeo and Juliet, before they kiss, takes the form of a sonnet, serving to complement the love between the pair and the profound nature of their connection as each delivers a line of the concluding couplet*.

A Summary of the Key Events in *Romeo and Juliet*

Prologue: The Chorus reveals that the children of two warring families fall in love and die, ending their parents' feud.

Act One

- **Scene 1:** The Prince stops a fight between the Montague and Capulet families. The son of Montague, Romeo, explains to his cousin Benvolio that he is depressed because of his unrequited love.
- **Scene 2:** The nobleman, Paris, asks Capulet for his daughter Juliet's hand in marriage. Capulet tells him that at thirteen she is too young, but he agrees to give his permission if Paris convinces Juliet. Capulet sends his servant, Peter, with a guest list for the night's ball. In the streets of Verona, Peter asks Benvolio and Romeo for help in reading the list. Realising that his love, Rosaline, is on the guest-list, Romeo decides to go to the ball.
- **Scene 3:** Juliet's nurse reminisces with Lady Capulet about Juliet's childhood. Lady Capulet tells Juliet about the marriage plans.
- **Scene 4:** Romeo, Mercutio and Benvolio discuss the ball as they make their way to it. Mercutio interrupts Romeo's account of a dream by describing the queen of the fairies: Queen Mab.
- **Scene 5:** Romeo sees Juliet. Tybalt recognises Romeo, and Capulet orders him to leave Romeo alone. Romeo and Juliet talk and kiss. Romeo and Juliet are informed by the Nurse that they belong to rival families.

Act Two

- **Prologue:** The Chorus summarises Act 1 and what will happen in this Act.
- **Scene 1:** Benvolio and Mercutio have lost Romeo. Mercutio calls to him with sarcastic and crass language.
- **Scene 2:** Romeo admires Juliet on her balcony. They tell each other of their love and agree to marry the next day.
- **Scene 3:** Friar Lawrence agrees to perform the marriage in the hope that it will reunite the two families.
- **Scene 4:** Mercutio and Benvolio discuss the fact that Tybalt has challenged Romeo to a duel. When Romeo arrives, his friends joke with him. Romeo tells the Nurse that Juliet should go to Friar Lawrence that afternoon to perform the marriage ceremony.
- **Scene 5:** The Nurse tells Juliet about the marriage arrangements.
- **Scene 6:** Juliet meets Romeo and Friar Lawrence at the Friar's cell.

Act Three

- **Scene 1:** While Tybalt is looking for Romeo, Mercutio attempts to pick a fight with him. Romeo arrives and Tybalt tries to pick a fight with Romeo but Romeo refuses. Mercutio fights Tybalt but is killed. Romeo kills Tybalt. The Prince banishes Romeo.
- **Scene 2:** The Nurse tells Juliet that Tybalt is dead and Romeo banished.
- **Scene 3:** Friar Lawrence tells Romeo that he is banished. The Nurse tells Romeo to go to Juliet.
- **Scene 4:** Capulet tells Paris that he may marry Juliet on Thursday.
- **Scene 5:** Romeo leaves Juliet, heading to Mantua. Juliet's parents are furious that she rejects the marriage to Paris. The Nurse advises Juliet to marry Paris and forget Romeo.

Act Four

- **Scene 1:** Paris discusses his approaching wedding with Friar Lawrence. When he leaves, Juliet asks the Friar for help, threatening suicide if he refuses. He gives her a potion that will make her appear dead. He says that her body will be taken to the family vault and he will tell Romeo to meet her there so that they can escape to Mantua together.
- **Scene 2:** Juliet apologises to her father and agrees to marry Paris. Capulet decides to hold the wedding a day earlier.
- **Scene 3:** Juliet drinks the potion.
- **Scene 4:** The next morning the Capulets prepare for the wedding.
- **Scene 5:** The Nurse cannot wake Juliet and informs everyone that she is dead. Friar Lawrence tries to calm everyone and tells them to take Juliet's body to the family vault.

Act Five

- **Scene 1:** Balthasar arrives in Mantua to inform Romeo of Juliet's death. Romeo buys poison from an apothecary so that he can travel to Juliet's grave and take his own life there.
- **Scene 2:** Friar John tells Friar Lawrence that he was unable to deliver Lawrence's message to Romeo. Friar Lawrence plans to move Juliet's body to his own cell.
- **Scene 3:** Paris visits Juliet in the vault. When Romeo arrives, Paris challenges him and is killed by Romeo. Romeo lies with Juliet, takes the poison and dies. Friar Lawrence finds the bodies of Romeo and Paris and as Juliet wakes, he tells her what has happened. Hearing a noise, the Friar tries to persuade Juliet to leave with him. She refuses and, after his departure, Juliet stabs herself with Romeo's dagger. Having been arrested, Friar Lawrence explains what has happened to the Prince, the Capulets and the Montagues. Montague and Capulet agree to end their feud.

Romeo and Juliet

25 Key Quotations for GCSE

Quotation 1

Act 1, Prologue

Prologue:

"A pair of star-crossed lovers take their life."

Analysis

The dramatic function of the Prologue supports a key theme of the play: fate. Within the space of fourteen lines, Shakespeare reveals the play's plot. The audience knows, before Act 1, scene 1 begins, the entire course of the narrative. The sense of inevitability that is conveyed by this knowledge supports the references to fate that dominate the play and reinforces Shakespeare's presentation of the power of fate. This also elevates the sense of tragedy as, throughout the narrative, the audience will be aware of the doomed nature of Romeo and Juliet's love. Compromising suspense by revealing the plot would not have been a major sacrifice to Shakespeare, as a significant proportion of his audience would have been familiar with the story through its earlier forms such as Bandello's novella, Brooke's narrative poem or the (now lost) play version. The Chorus was a dramatic device frequently employed in Classical Greek tragedy; it was used to comment on the action without participating in it. By using a Chorus here, Shakespeare could be elevating the seriousness and significance of his tragedy; his constructs of Romeo and Juliet are raised to the status of mythical characters from the Classics, whose futures are determined by fate rather than their actions.

This quotation is part of the sonnet* that constitutes the form of the Prologue. Brooke's poem, *The Tragicall Historie of Romeus and Juliet*, that Shakespeare used as source material for his play, also begins with a sonnet. Sonnets are conventionally associated with love and so help to convey the central theme of the play. The regularity of a sonnet's rhyme scheme, length and meter also reinforce the theme of fate, as the regularity of the structure conveys a sense of inevitability and a set pattern. The Petrarchan* sonnet (the traditional sonnet form) frequently exploits the idea of love at first sight, the rejection of a lover and their resulting melancholy. These themes are all employed by Shakespeare in the play.

'Star-crossed' literally means 'opposed by the stars'. Many Elizabethans believed that the stars controlled fate. Given that the previous line refers to the birth of the lovers ('From forth the fatal loins') it appears that Shakespeare is suggesting that the 'pair' are doomed from birth. Fate is against them from their very conception. The word 'crossed' is ambiguous* and could be read as an implicit allusion* to crucifixion, with its connotations* of Christ's sacrifice; perhaps Romeo and Juliet can be seen to be sacrificial victims of their families' feud. This ambiguity continues in the phrase 'take their life'; the most obvious interpretation is that this refers to the death of the two lovers through suicide, yet the phrase could also refer back to the birth of the characters from the 'fatal loins' of their warring parents. This binary opposition between life and death is frequently represented by Shakespeare throughout the play, as are many other oppositions which convey the intensity of the conflict between the Montagues and Capulets.

Key Characters

Juliet
Romeo

Key Themes

Death
Fate and Love

Quotation 2

Act 1, Scene 1

Sampson:

"My naked weapon is out. Quarrel, I will back thee."

Analysis

The conflict that exists between the Capulet and Montague families dominates the play. The family feud is represented as the obstacle for Romeo and Juliet's relationship. Shakespeare's exposition foregrounds this conflict through the minor characters of Sampson and Gregory. The representation of these characters' immature behaviour may serve to dramatically position the audience's response to the conflict, conveying it to be ridiculous.

Sampson and Gregory, as representatives of the house of Capulet, are immediately presented as comedic through their excessive machismo, false bravado and crude innuendo. The comic nature of their characterisation makes the conflict seem absurd and pointless. Sampson's boast 'My naked weapon is out,' follows a series of sexual puns that clarify that this reference to his sword is also an allusion to his penis. The adjective 'naked' suggests that Sampson is playfully exploiting the ambiguity in Gregory's instruction that Sampson should 'Draw thy tool'. The metaphorically* 'naked' weapon refers back to his claim, moments before, that when he has fought the Montague men, he would cut off '...the heads of the maids, or their maidenheads...', taking the virginity of the Montague women. There is a blurring of the boundaries between sex and violence that is both absurd and disturbing, with this idea of inappropriateness extending to the conflict between the Montagues and Capulets as a whole.

When Shakespeare wrote the play, the middle classes were growing and wished to have the status symbols associated with the aristocracy; one of these symbols was a sword. A growing number of people carrying weapons in urban areas was a significant issue for public safety, so rules of conduct were created. It is the uncertainty regarding these rules that Shakespeare may be parodying* in Sampson's frequent queries regarding the law that governs his actions in this part of the scene.

Sampson's use of the imperative* verb 'Quarrel' illustrates his desire to provoke conflict whilst being hesitant about his own involvement. He instructs Gregory to begin an argument, promising to support him with his 'I will back thee'. Even Gregory, his fellow Capulet, questions Sampson's bravery here through the homographic pun* on the word 'back'. While Sampson uses the word figuratively, to mean 'support', Gregory uses it literally, suggesting that Sampson will turn his back to the fight and run away. Once again, in representing the immaturity of the characters, Shakespeare provides comedy through the repeated wordplay, whilst also highlighting the ridiculous nature of the feud.

Key Characters

The Capulets

Key Themes

Conflict

Excess

Quotation 3

Act 1, Scene 1

Tybalt:

"...peace? I hate the word / As I hate hell, all Montagues, and thee."

Analysis

Shakespeare employs cratylic naming* with the presentation of the character of Benvolio, whose name means 'of good will'. Benvolio immediately lives up to his name by drawing his sword in an attempt to stop the fight. Tybalt, in contrast, is presented as aggressive, immediately challenging Benvolio to a fight. The name 'Tybalt' contrasts the character with the cowardice evident in Sampson and Gregory given that it is derived, etymologically*, from 'brave people'. However, Tybalt's bravery is not bound by honour or sense; he is a creature of passion rather than reason so that his response to the reasonable request of Benvolio to put away the sword or use it to help him stop the fight, is mocked through his condemnation of 'peace'.

Shakespeare employs a tripartite* list for the elements that Tybalt hates, the effect being to highlight the extent of Tybalt's hatred. The first item in the list, 'hell' with its obvious religious connotations of a place of evil, suffering and torture, is an accepted focus of hatred but to apply this degree of negative emotion to 'peace' seems ridiculous. To present the concept of 'peace' as negative, given its highly positive connotations, allows Shakespeare to establish Tybalt as a character who is determined to fight and who wishes to maintain the division and hostility in Verona.

The reference to 'all Montagues' reveals the indiscriminate nature of his hatred for the Montague family. To equate his hatred of hell with 'all Montagues, and thee' suggests that Tybalt regards the Montagues as being as despicable and negative as 'hell'; he is quite willing to target a well-intentioned Benvolio with this same hatred. Tybalt's hot temper contrasts the concern shown, even by immature characters like Sampson and Gregory, who show some reluctance to break the law. Tybalt has no such qualms. He forces Benvolio into an unwanted fight, perhaps foreshadowing* the way in which he will later draw Romeo into an unwanted fight, with tragic consequences. Shakespeare's representation of Tybalt portrays the potential dangers of excessive emotion. His presence on stage is unsettling for an audience, given his volatility.

Key Characters

Benvolio

Tybalt

Key Themes

Conflict

Excess

Family

Religion

Quotation 4

Act 1, Scene 1

Romeo:

"O brawling love, O loving hate... / O heavy lightness... / Feather of lead, bright smoke, cold fire, sick health!"

Analysis

Romeo's series of exclamations may be used by Shakespeare to present Romeo as experiencing an excess of emotion. Romeo is, initially, represented as a stereotype of a Petrarchan lover; his love is expressed in grand language, using rhyme and oxymorons* that may convey the conflicting emotions of unrequited love. However, Shakespeare may be representing the artificial, immature love of Romeo in these terms so that it acts as a contrast to the true love he experiences with Juliet, a love that is conveyed through blank verse* rather than the old-fashioned and artificial form found in Petrarchan verse.

The frequency of the oxymorons in such close proximity complements the hyperbolic* nature of Romeo's emotions. Shakespeare conveys a sense of emotional immaturity through the extreme contrasts and logical inconsistencies caused by oxymoronic language. Just as the phrases are incompatible, logically, Shakespeare could be suggesting that Romeo and Rosaline may be incompatible lovers.

An alternative interpretation is that Romeo may not be referring to his love for Rosaline. While he begins by referring to his unrequited love, his reflections are interrupted by spotting the disorder caused by the fight that has just ended. The love that he refers to, in this interpretation, is the love of family that creates profound loyalty and leads to conflict with those who do not share this bond of love. Hence the fight between the Montagues and Capulets is a 'brawling love' because it is a love that causes conflict. The series of oxymorons may be read as a parody* of Petrarchan ideas, with Romeo illustrating the conflict in Verona and how love can lead to hate, a motif* that is explored throughout the play. Romeo could be represented as criticising Benvolio for his part in the 'fray'.

Romeo's representation of love is both relatable and intriguing for an audience. Love is a universally experienced emotion and ambivalent feelings are common when one is in love. The semantic field* of illness (in the oxymoron 'sick health!') conveys a sense of the physical 'symptoms' a lover might experience. The main effect of Romeo's oxymoronic dialogue is to demonstrate the overwhelming and confusing nature of love. An audience's sympathy for the protagonists develops as we are reminded (through watching the spectacle on stage) of the young age of these inexperienced lovers.

Key Characters

Romeo

Key Themes

Conflict

Excess

Love

Quotation 5

Act 1, Scene 2

Capulet:

"She's the hopeful lady of my earth."

Analysis

The scene begins with Paris asking Lord Capulet for his consent to marry Juliet. It seems that Capulet is presented as a concerned parent who respects Juliet's role in such a decision. Shakespeare stresses, at this early stage in the play, that Juliet is only 13 years old, having 'not seen the change of fourteen years,' and her value to Capulet is explored here. While, at this early point, her father seems to demonstrate love and respect for his daughter, there is also a sense that she is a commodity to be won by Paris. A major difference in Elizabethan wedding customs (compared with marriages today) was that a woman would have had little choice in terms of her potential husband. Marriages were frequently arranged for financial benefit and so this subtle representation of Juliet as a commodity to be won would have been a reality for many Elizabethans.

Unlike the rest of Capulet's speech, this line does not form part of a rhyming couplet, which potentially has the effect of foregrounding its importance for an audience. Capulet may be figuratively referring to Juliet as his progeny who has grown from his own soil ('my earth'). Perhaps Shakespeare intended to use the word 'earth' to mean body, as he did in Sonnet 146: 'Poor soul, the centre of my sinful earth.'

The ambiguous nature of Capulet's language use is evident in Shakespeare's repetition of the words 'earth' and 'hope'. In the previous line, the 'earth', in a literal sense, is described as having 'swallow'd all my hopes but she.' It seems that Capulet's other children have all died and are buried beneath the earth.

Capulet may also be referring to 'earth' literally, as he did in the line before. In this sense he may be alluding to his own death, when he is 'in the earth'. The adjective 'hopeful' may be applied to both Capulet and Juliet. He hopes for a prosperous and powerful continuation of the Capulet family line through his sole remaining child. The adjective 'hopeful' could also apply to Juliet's character, depicting her as a positive force in his life. The declarative nature of Capulet's dialogue ('she *is* ...') conveys a sense that his fatherly expectations for Juliet are excessive, given that he appears to place unreasonable focus on his daughter to fulfil his own hopes.

Given the Prologue's previous revelation, the audience may recognise a degree of dramatic irony* in Capulet's words, as Juliet will soon be confined to the earth, when she dies. Certainly, Shakespeare is, once again, juxtaposing the themes of love and death, an idea raised moments before in scene 1 when Romeo imagines Rosaline's death.

Key Characters

Capulet

Juliet

Paris

Key Themes

Family

Fate

Love

Quotation 6

Act 1, Scene 4

Romeo:
"Some consequence yet hanging in the stars."

Analysis

The discussion of dreams that is dominated by Mercutio's 'Queen Mab' speech, gives Romeo a premonition of death. Shakespeare frequently uses imagery of death and foreshadowing in the play. However, here he allows the character of Romeo to explicitly refer to his own 'untimely death'. Dramatic irony is produced here by Shakespeare: the audience is made omniscient through the Prologue's revelations and understands the tragic reality of Romeo's fate, while he does not. The imagery of the cosmos mirrors that used in the Prologue, helping to ensure that the audience appreciates that the 'consequence yet hanging in the stars' links directly to the doomed 'star-crossed lovers'.

Later in the play, Romeo and Juliet refer to each other through the language of the cosmos. This allows Shakespeare to draw parallels between love, death and fate as the images are filled with significance from a variety of scenes. Even before his explicit references to death, the 'consequence' here is figuratively connected to death as the verb 'hanging' has such powerful connotations of unnatural death.

While the audience has some appreciation of Romeo's fate, Romeo's own concerns are logically grounded in the feud between the Montagues and Capulets. He, the heir to the Montagues, is about to enter the house of his family's greatest enemies. Given the street-fight between the Montagues and Capulets earlier that day, Romeo's concerns would be legitimate. However, it is ironic that Romeo's death will only indirectly be a result of the feud between the warring families and that love will be central to his death.

Ultimately, Romeo offers himself to a personified Fate. 'He that hath the steerage of my course / Direct my sail,' suggests that Romeo sees himself as powerless in governing his own future, a fatalistic* belief that was shared by many Elizabethans in the sixteenth century.

Key Characters

Romeo

Key Themes

Death

Fate

Love

Quotation 7

Act 1, Scene 5

Romeo:

"...she hangs upon the cheek of night / As a rich jewel in an Ethiop's ear"

Analysis

Romeo's immaturity and fickle nature is clear in the love that he shows for Juliet, as soon as he catches sight of her. His impulsive nature is made even more evident given the context of this speech; he is attending the Capulet ball in an effort to see his 'love', Rosaline. Once again, the language and the form in which the love is expressed is hyperbolic and poetic, presenting Romeo as a stereotypical Petrarchan lover. The use of rhyming couplets makes Romeo's comments seem artificial, perhaps illustrating the artificial nature of love based on superficial attraction.

Romeo immediately associates Juliet with the light, a key motif within the play. The hyperbolic claim that her brightness is so powerful that 'she doth teach the torches to burn bright' is extended in the conceit* of her as a 'jewel' in an 'Ethiop's ear'. 'Ethiop' was a term used by Elizabethans for anyone who appeared dark-skinned, so the colour contrast is far more important than the country referenced. This brightness is exaggerated through the contrast between the glittering jewel that she is chremamorphically* identified as and the dark Ethiopian skin that the night is personified through. Women in the second half of the 1500s increasingly wore earrings, once the fashion for headwear that covered the ears ended. These earrings frequently included pearls, the lustre and whiteness of which, serves Shakespeare's imagery particularly well.

The conceit is one that Shakespeare used in sonnet 27: 'Which, like a jewel hung in ghastly night, Makes black night beauteous and her old face new', representing the transformative effect of the imagination just as here, Juliet shines out of the darkness of the Capulet throng to transform Romeo's experience. The image of the 'ghastly night' used in the sonnet is transformed, here, into 'the cheek of night', something soft and intimate that serves to convey Romeo's tender thoughts. Still, the links between love and death are subtly alluded to through Shakespeare's use of the verb 'hung'.

Juliet's value is also conveyed through the jewel metaphor*. The connotations of a jewel with high value is emphasised through Romeo's modification of 'jewel' with the adjective 'rich'. It is interesting that Shakespeare chooses to convey Romeo's initial admiration of Juliet through the language of objectification, reminding the audience of his superficial emotions.

Key Characters

Juliet

Romeo

Key Themes

Love

Quotation 8

Act 1, Scene 5

Romeo:

"If I profane with my unworthiest hand / This holy shrine, the gentle sin is this, / My lips, two blushing pilgrims, ready stand"

Analysis

The first words spoken by Romeo to Juliet form the first quatrain* of a sonnet. The dialogue that takes place before the couple kiss, consists of 14 lines of rhymed iambic pentameter, making it a perfectly constructed English sonnet. This form is conventionally associated with love and therefore conveys that genuine love is evident between Romeo and Juliet. The fact that the words of both lovers are required to complete the sonnet may help to convey that the love is reciprocated, unlike the feelings of Romeo for Rosaline. There is an immediate sense that Romeo and Juliet complete each other in the same way that their words complete the sonnet form.

The significance of the meeting between Romeo and Juliet being presented through the conceit of Romeo as a pilgrim is stressed by Shakespeare's choice of cratylic naming. 'Romeo' is a later form of the Italian 'Romei' meaning a pilgrim who travels to the holy sites of Rome. Romeo's name therefore defines him as a pilgrim, and he identifies Juliet as the site of his pilgrimage.

The semantic field of religion is exploited throughout the play, but it is particularly important here. Romeo elevates his feelings for Juliet to a spiritual level, presenting her as sacred and claiming that his own hand would profane her through its touch – to touch her is a sacrilegious act; he flatters her by elevating her status and presents himself humbly by undermining his own value through the superlative adjective 'unworthiest'. However, Romeo immediately subverts the sense of being unworthy by extending the religious conceit, dismissing his hand but offering his lips, presenting them as a means of atoning for the sin of touching her sacred form. This act draws upon the conventional practice of pilgrims who would kiss a shrine in an effort to remove their sins. He uses the simile* of his lips as 'pilgrims' who have come expressly to worship at the shrine of her hand. The swift shift from self-deprecation to the offer of his lips through the same religious conceit suggests that Romeo is using language to seduce.

'Blushing' connotes an innocence belied by Romeo's wordplay but also suggests the redness of his own lips, presenting them as inviting, elevating himself.

Key Characters

Juliet
Romeo

Key Themes

Love
Religion

Quotation 9

Act 1, Scene 5

Juliet:

"My only love sprung from my only hate!"

Analysis

The intensity of the meeting between Romeo and Juliet is evident in that neither of them initially think to ask the other's name. Romeo enquires after Juliet's name from the Nurse and later Juliet seeks knowledge of Romeo from the Nurse as well.

The fatalistic tragedy of the play is evident in Juliet's exclamation: 'My only love sprung from my only hate!' The exclamatory* form conveys the depth of her dismay. Antithetical parallelism* may represent the link that Juliet creates between these two extreme emotions. The parallelism complements the sense of these two opposing emotions being inextricably linked. Romeo cannot change his family and Juliet cannot change her love. Their relationship is doomed by Fate.

The adjective 'only' illustrates how Juliet's strong emotions are limited and focused in a way that is in stark contrast to those of her cousin Tybalt, who claims to hate peace, '...hell, all

Montagues, and thee.' Applying the adjective 'only' to 'love' could indicate that this is Juliet's first love – she is, after all, only thirteen. However, it could also represent a recognition of the intensity of this feeling. Juliet believes that this will be her only love, a belief that the audience would appreciate, through dramatic irony, as being true as a result of her imminent death. Using 'only' to refer to her hate again focuses the audience's attention on the limited nature of Juliet's emotions, generating sympathy for her as Fate seems cruel in selecting her one true love from the one hate that she was born to hold.

The verb 'sprung' has connotations of natural and new life, given that it functions as the past participle of 'spring' but, more importantly, it conveys the impulsive and sudden nature of this love. Juliet has rapidly changed from not knowing Romeo to loving him and understanding the tragic nature of his background.

Key Characters

Juliet

Key Themes

Conflict

Family

Love

Quotation 10

Act 2, Scene 2

Romeo:

"It is the east, and Juliet is the sun. / Arise, fair sun, and kill the envious moon..."

Analysis

The balcony scene begins with Romeo seeing a light at Juliet's window. Romeo and Juliet's love is presented, throughout the play, as flourishing at night, perhaps providing a means for Shakespeare to remind his audience of the elicit nature of their love. This speech allows Shakespeare to again associate Juliet with light and brightness. The reference to 'the east' identifies Juliet's room as the source of the light in the same way that the east is identified as the source of the sunrise. Juliet is therefore represented not only as the sun but the sun as it rises, dispelling the darkness and bringing new life to the world. The sun is associated with power, warmth and beauty, qualities that Romeo's metaphor ascribes to Juliet. In addition to these flattering connotations, Romeo modifies the sun as 'fair', drawing specific attention to Juliet's beauty through the metaphor. The imperative verb 'arise' supports the metaphor of Juliet as the sun, linking the image of the sun rising to Juliet literally rising from her bed.

In Act 1, scene 2, when referring to Rosaline, Romeo states: 'the all-seeing sun / Ne'er saw her match'. This flattery of Rosaline is undermined by this point in the play as Romeo metaphorically identifies Juliet with this omniscient celestial body. While Rosaline may have been an earthly beauty, Juliet is heavenly. In Act 1, scene 1 Romeo complains about Rosaline having 'Dian's wit', a reference to the Roman goddess of virginity, personified as the moon. His complaint centres on Rosaline refusing to give her virginity to him. In this scene, Romeo implores the sun, figuratively representing Juliet, to kill the moon. This could be interpreted as a plea for Juliet to lose her virginity to him, destroying the moon that represents the goddess of virginity, which is itself jealous of her beauty. It could also allude to the rejection of Rosaline, a chaste figure who, while beautiful, could only be envious of Juliet's beauty. Romeo's feelings for Juliet are far more powerful than those he held for Rosaline; the former 'outshines' the latter.

Key Characters

Juliet

Romeo

Key Themes

Love

Quotation 11

Act 2, Scene 2

Juliet:

"O Romeo, Romeo, wherefore art thou Romeo?
Deny thy father and refuse thy name…"

Analysis

Juliet's opening words are expressed through the archaic* exclamation 'O', highlighting the depth of her feeling. Her speech is a rhetorical apostrophe*, an exclamatory speech addressed to someone who is not there. While Romeo is present, Juliet is not aware of this and addresses him only in order to explore her ideas regarding him.

Her repetition of 'Romeo' three times in single sentence draws audience attention to the significance of his name, rendering the command for him to refuse his name even more difficult to imagine as achievable.

Juliet is trying to resolve the issue of her only love coming from her only hate by wishing that Romeo would reject his Montague name. 'Wherefore', meaning 'why', suggests that Juliet is distraught because of the situation that Fate has placed her in. The difficulty of this is further suggested by proposing the imperative clause 'Deny thy father' before 'refuse thy name'; this is not a simple process but one that would require the denial of family; what Juliet requires of Romeo would, she knows, demand the rejection of those closest to him and placing the clause 'Deny thy father' before 'refuse thy name' reveals that Juliet understands the significance of her wishes as well as the difficulty of Romeo being able to fulfil them. She is represented as mature and thoughtful, characteristics that belie her years.

The reaction of Romeo to Juliet's opening words offers significant scope for directorial choice since the direct address provided by the rhetorical apostrophe provides an opportunity for comedy; Romeo could be presented as believing himself to be addressed directly. Also, the intimacy of Romeo with the audience through the asides* that surround Juliet's speech, help to make the audience complicit in Romeo's eavesdropping, making the speech even more dramatically powerful.

Key Characters

Juliet
Romeo
The Montagues

Key Themes

Conflict
Family
Fate
Love

Quotation 12

Act 2, Scene 2

Juliet:

"That which we call a rose / By any other name would smell as sweet"

Analysis

Juliet continues to reflect on the nature of existence, to persuade herself that it is possible to love Romeo. She claims that Romeo himself is not the issue; the only issue is the name used to denote him. She follows Romeo's aside with ''Tis but thy name that is my enemy' and Shakespeare focuses on the significance of naming in what follows. It is interesting that the first quarto* uses the phrase 'By any other name' while the second quarto uses 'By any other word.' Given the focus on Romeo's family name of Montague, the first quarto's choice may be more compelling.

It is entirely appropriate that Shakespeare uses the example of the rose to convey the insignificance of naming, given that the flower is clearly associated with love. This association is based on a Classical Greek myth in which Chloris transforms a dead nymph into a flower that Aphrodite dedicates to her son, Eros, the god of love, naming it 'Rose'. For Juliet to select this example, illustrates that her mind is preoccupied with thoughts of love.

Similarly, Juliet focuses on a positive quality of the rose: the sweet smell. The implication is that Romeo exhibits positive qualities and that these would continue no matter what name was given to him. The positivity is reinforced by the phonologically* smooth quality of this phrase, created by the use of three sibilant* sounds within the words 'smell as sweet'.

Some claim that the choice of a rose for Juliet's example could be a subtle historical allusion to the Wars of the Roses. Shakespeare was certainly very interested in the war, having written History plays on the subject before the production of *Romeo and Juliet* and the war itself has parallels with the narrative of the play. Two warring families, York (white rose) and Lancaster (red rose) engaged in conflict for many years, causing the unnecessary deaths of members of their lines and those associated with them. Shakespeare's interest in the narrative of Brooke's *The Tragicall History of Romeus and Juliet*, could be, in part, what he perceived to be the possibility of allegorical* interpretation.

Key Characters

Juliet

Romeo

Key Themes

Conflict

Family

Love

Quotation 13

Act 2, Scene 2

Juliet:

"It is too rash, too unadvis'd, too sudden,
Too like the lightning"

Analysis

Juliet's maturity, in contrast to Romeo's, is evident once again. While Romeo is intent on swearing his love for her, Juliet pauses him, wishing him to be more considered. There may be a sense of foreboding here. Juliet could be concerned that what began quickly could end quickly. The dramatic irony produced by the Prologue's revelation of the play's tragic conclusion should confirm that Juliet's concerns are well-placed. The same foreboding is shown by Romeo in his reply to Benvolio's comment that they may be late for the Capulet ball: 'I fear too early, for my mind misgives some consequence.'

Romeo is reckless and driven by poetic passion. When Juliet is concerned for his safety, within the walls of the Capulet estate, Romeo states, 'With love's light wings did I o'erperch these walls.' While she is practical, he is fanciful. His determination to swear his love by the moon, or anything else, is countered by Juliet's considered approach.

Juliet's concerns are presented through a variety of literary techniques. The list of objections is asyndetic*, providing a sense of the list being endless, as are the objections to the speed of their romance. This is complemented by the parallelism of the first few clauses, each including an intensifier* followed by an adjective. The syntactic similarity gives a sense of each different idea being linked; the romance is impetuous, ill-considered and swift, all of which pose rational obstacles to a meaningful declaration of love.

The intensifier 'too' conveys excess; Juliet accepts the profound nature of the emotions felt by them both, but the excessive emotions are a potential barrier to a successful relationship, and this is emphasised through the repetition of the word, making its very articulation excessive. Even the meter of the line complements the sense of excess, with Shakespeare adding an extra syllable to the line, over-extending it.

The concluding simile of lightning represents love as potentially brief; it is dramatic and startling but transitory. Lightning is bright but disappears before, 'one can say "It lightens"', a stark contrast to the enduring power of the sun that Romeo likens Juliet to at the beginning of the scene.

Key Characters

Juliet
Romeo

Key Themes

Excess
Family
Love

Quotation 14

Act 2, Scene 3

Friar Lawrence:

"Wisely and slow; they stumble that run fast."

Analysis

The philosophy presented by the Friar, a form of the Latin idiom* 'Festina lente' (make haste slowly), complements the wisdom shown in Juliet's 'too rash' speech in Act 2, scene 2.

There is wisdom in the Friar's words, and he appears as a character who wishes to do good, yet he fails to heed his own sage advice. In swiftly agreeing to perform the marriage ceremony that same day, he will inevitably 'stumble'. The attempt to heal the division between the Montagues and Capulets through marriage is a reasonable one given that, in the period in which the play is set, many divided families were brought together through marriage. To unite the only surviving children of the Montagues and Capulets would seem a chance that Friar Lawrence cannot resist, even if this means rejecting the possibility of performing it 'Wisely and slow'. In fact, Friar Lawrence's error lies in the way he performs his services to Romeo and Juliet. Without proper notice and ceremony, the marriage is hidden, and deceit governs all the events which follow, leading to tragedy.

The metaphor of running and the potential for injury caused by a 'stumble', foreshadows the many deaths that will occur as a result of the 'haste' in Romeo and Juliet's relationship.

The final section of the scene, that concludes in this quotation, takes the form of a sonnet, subtly conveying love to be the subject in form as well as language. The fact that the Friar sometimes completes Romeo's lines of iambic pentameter, as well as the pair of them contributing to the completion of the sonnet, suggests their intimate connection. The Friar fulfils the role of both a teacher and a father-figure to Romeo.

The stichomythia* that is evident in this pseudo-sonnet section serves to reinforce the sense of haste felt by the characters and makes the Friar's concluding remarks rather ironic. Neither he, nor Romeo, have been 'slow' and the structure conveys this.

Key Characters

Friar Lawrence

Key Themes

Excess

Family

Love

Quotation 15

Act 2, Scene 6

Friar Lawrence:

"These violent delights have violent ends,
And in their triumph die like fire and powder."

Analysis

From a practical dramatic perspective, time needs to pass on stage before Juliet can enter for the marriage ceremony, as she was on stage at the end of scene 5. As a result, Shakespeare uses the opportunity for Friar Lawrence and Romeo to discuss the nature of Romeo's love, whilst providing time for the character of Juliet to realistically appear.

The wedding scene is very short and the ceremony itself is not staged. While a comedy might be expected to end with a wedding, this scene marks the play's turning-point into tragedy; this is alluded to through the frequent juxtaposition* of images of death/violence to love/marriage within the scene.

The Friar's words are a response to Romeo's urgency. Romeo prophetically claims that death can do its work if he can just be married to Juliet. The Friar asks for his patience, as he did in Act 2, scene 3's 'Wisely slow'. The parallelism of 'violent delights have violent ends' joins these seemingly contrasting points, making the link between them appear inevitable. If Romeo loves quickly, this passion may end quickly. This echoes the caution shown by Juliet in Act 2, scene 2. Shakespeare may be using a homographic pun on the word 'violent'. The modern understanding of the word's denotation* fits the play's tragic conclusion as both lovers die through acts of violence towards themselves, but the word is derived from the Latin 'violentia' which denotes impetuosity. The idea of impetuosity certainly fits the kind of love that Romeo has displayed for Rosaline and now, it seems to the Friar, for Juliet.

The parallelism seems oxymoronic* given that 'violent ends' seems to metaphorically refer to death while 'violent delights' appears to rather euphemistically refer to Romeo's physical passion. The Friar suggests that an uncontrolled and swift passion can ultimately mean that this passion is short-lived. The irony of this, in terms of the imminent deaths of Romeo and Juliet, is unlikely to be lost on the audience.

The simile draws a comparison between the bright and intense heat of fire and gunpowder when combined, and intense passion. The result is powerful, overwhelming and dangerous but, once again, short-lived.

Key Characters

Friar Lawrence

Key Themes

Death

Love

Quotation 16

Act 3, Scene 1

Mercutio:

"A plague o'both your houses!"

Analysis

Mercutio is neither a Montague nor a Capulet. His curse foreshadows the devastation of the two families in the loss of their only heirs. Mercutio's curse is indiscriminate. He feels wronged by Tybalt, the Capulet and his friend Romeo, the Montague. To Mercutio, Romeo has betrayed his honour by failing to meet the demands of conventional masculine behaviour of the time: he does not fight when provoked. To add injury to insult, when Mercutio steps in to defend Romeo's honour, Romeo's attempt to stop the duel inadvertently allows Mercutio to be stabbed.

Mercutio repeats the curse three times before his exit. A widespread Elizabethan belief was that a curse only became effective when it was uttered for the third time. Someone could utter a curse as a joke but using it a second time revealed their seriousness, while a third would damn the object of the curse. Shakespeare characterises Mercutio as a joker and Romeo understandably believes him to be joking when he reveals that he has been hurt, having received 'a scratch'. The second use of the curse serves to establish Mercutio's seriousness and the recognition that his death may be a result of the feud between the Montagues and Capulets.

To curse the houses of Montague and Capulet with the plague would have been profoundly disturbing at the time; the plague was a real threat in the sixteenth century. Various plague outbreaks had occurred throughout the century, with one taking place between 1592-1593, just before Shakespeare wrote the play. The 1563 attack of the plague, alone, killed a quarter of London's population. Those who contracted the plague only had a 50% chance of survival and symptoms were horrific.

It is worth noting that the failure of Friar Lawrence's letter to reach Romeo and, therefore, a cause of both Romeo and Juliet's deaths, is that Friar John was prevented from leaving a house infested with the plague (Act 5, scene 2). In this sense, a plague has caused the destruction of both houses.

Shakespeare uses ellipsis* in Mercutio's final words in the play, removing an element of his curse. Both the curse and the meter of the line are cut short, as is Mercutio's life, with the words 'Your houses!'

Key Characters

Mercutio

Key Themes

Conflict

Death

Family

Quotation 17

Act 3, Scene 1

Mercutio:

"Ask for me tomorrow, and you shall find me a grave man"

Analysis

Mercutio is a character who is both comedic and unpredictable. Throughout the first two acts he has used a variety of puns and sexual innuendo with his Queen Mab speech demonstrating that his wit can also have a more profound quality.

Once again, Shakespeare appears to have engaged in cratylic naming. 'Mercutio' is derived from the Latin form for 'Mercury'. Mercury was used as a cure for syphilis in the sixteenth century, making this an appropriate association for someone whose speech so frequently uses sexual puns and innuendo. Mercury was the name of the Roman god of messengers and tricksters; Mercutio's role as a trickster is evident whenever he appears but as a character who is neither a Capulet nor a Montague, he also acts as a transition (or messenger role) between the warring families: he is the character who is friends with the Montagues yet is invited to the Capulet ball. Finally, as an element, Mercury was known for its volatility, making the name entirely appropriate for Mercutio's unpredictable character.

Mercutio speaks in prose and various forms of verse throughout the opening of the play; his unpredictability is evident in not being bound by the conventions* of verse. At this point in the play he speaks in prose, perhaps indicating the fundamental nature of his concerns.

Even though Mercutio recognises his imminent death he still exhibits his wit using the homographic pun 'grave man'. Like Mercury (also known as Quicksilver), Mercutio's mind is swift, and the audience is likely to admire and appreciate the clever and entertaining wordplay. 'Grave', meaning 'serious', could imply that now he is injured, Mercutio will cease his joking but the cause of this is clear in the more common denotation of the word 'grave'– he will be entombed within his grave, following his death.

In Italy the funeral would usually take place very soon after death to avoid the ill-effects of the heat on the body, perhaps explaining why Mercutio would refer to 'Tomorrow'. An audience that recognises the implications of Mercutio's words would, perhaps appreciate both the comic and tragic nature of his words.

The death of Mercutio is not included in Shakespeare's source material so is clearly significant to Shakespeare, perhaps because of the way in which it illustrates the wider impact of the feud between the Montagues and Capulets.

Key Characters

Mercutio

Key Themes

Conflict

Death

Family

Quotation 18

Act 3, Scene 2

Juliet:

"...when I shall die, / Take him and cut him out in little stars"

Analysis

There is a lot of critical debate regarding whether the pronoun 'he' or 'I' should be used in the first clause of this quotation. The second quarto of 1599 uses 'I', as does the third of 1609. It is only with the production of the fourth quarto of 1622 that 'he' is used instead. The pronoun 'he' seems to make more logical sense given that cutting Romeo up would require his death and the idea of this being necessary because of Juliet's death (if using the pronoun 'I') seems uncharacteristically selfish of Juliet. However, it is necessary to appreciate the context of this utterance in order to understand its possible interpretations.

Most readings treat this statement as a romantic expression of Juliet's love. Romeo's beauty is such that Juliet elevates it to a celestial level. His beauty will transform the heavens as she imagines him as a constellation of stars, appreciated by everyone. Juliet makes the personal universal, the love between Romeo and Juliet having macrocosmic* significance. Just as Romeo is made universal by being metaphorically represented as stars, the night which holds these stars is rendered more personal and intimate through personification*; it is 'gentle night' and Romeo will make the 'face of heaven so fine.' It could be argued that Juliet is infantilised by Shakespeare through the imagery used at this point. She is still only 13 years old and the image of 'cutting out little stars' as well as the use of the diminutive* 'little' serves to remind the audience of her youth and innocence, something that she does herself through her reference to 'an impatient child'. This makes the play all the more tragic as the audience know both the fate of the 'star-crossed lovers' (alluded to through the star imagery) and, through dramatic irony, that this high point of Juliet's happiness and her romantic vision is about to collapse as a result of Romeo having killed Tybalt.

However, it is possible to read this speech as a reference to sex rather than a child-like romantic vision. Juliet's soliloquy* is dominated by her anticipation of losing her virginity. She longs for Romeo to come to her so that she can be 'possess'd' and the word 'die' was commonly used by Elizabethans as a euphemism* to refer to sexual climax. In this context, therefore, the use of the pronoun 'I' would be entirely appropriate. Juliet imagines the moment of her own sexual fulfilment ('when I die') transforming Romeo into a heavenly body worthy of 'worship'.

Key Characters

Juliet

Romeo

Key Themes

Fate

Love

Quotation 19

Act 3, Scene 2

Juliet:

"Beautiful tyrant, fiend angelical!
Dove-feather'd raven, wolvish-ravening lamb!"

Analysis

Having been told by the Nurse that Romeo is responsible for the death of her cousin, Tybalt, Juliet states: 'O serpent heart, hid with a flow'ring face!' an allusion to the idea of evil and danger being hidden by beautiful appearances. This was a favourite theme of Shakespeare's that he returned to in plays like *Macbeth*: 'look like the innocent flower but be the serpent under it,' and *Hamlet* 'O tiger's heart wrapt in a woman's hide!' Juliet briefly regards Romeo as deceitful because of this duality of his nature. This is conveyed through the series of oxymorons that follow. The tension that exists within oxymorons also reflects the tension within Juliet's ambivalent feelings for Romeo: she loves him and hates what he has done.

'Beautiful tyrant' mirrors the effect of 'serpent heart, hid with a flow'ring face' in that it focuses on the distinction between outward appearance and the evil nature that it hides. As with all oxymorons, it conveys that something is very wrong as the words create a logical tension. The reference to the serpent in the preceding line connotes temptation in the Garden of Eden and is therefore associated with evil acts. This is continued in 'fiend angelical'. 'Fiend' is a term to denote Satan, so to describe the fiend as 'angelical', appears oxymoronic and maintains the effect of other oxymorons in this sequence. However, the phrase could also be read more literally; Satan was an angel and Shakespeare could be focusing on Juliet's sense of having been deceived by Romeo. 2 Corinthians states 'Satan himself masquerades as an angel of light.'

'Dove-feather'd raven' refers to a white raven, a black bird with white feathers and, therefore, a false creature. The choice of birds may also act as a Biblical allusion. They are the two birds released by Noah following the Flood, according to Genesis. Yet another Biblical allusion is evident in 'wolvish-ravening lamb'. The adjective 'wolvish' seems entirely inconsistent with 'lamb' and is, therefore, an effective oxymoron but it also alludes to Matthew 7, verse 15: 'Beware of false prophets, which come to you in sheep's clothing, but inwardly they are ravening wolves.' Romeo's courtship of Juliet was couched in religious imagery and language so to use religious language to convey the way in which she feels deceived by Romeo may represent how Juliet now feels that the original courtship was suspect.

It is worth noting that these doubts last no longer than speech itself.

Key Characters

Juliet

Romeo

Key Themes

Conflict

Love

Quotation 20

Act 3, Scene 3

Romeo:

"In what vile part of this anatomy / Doth my name lodge? Tell me, that I may sack / The hateful mansion."

Analysis

The first half of scene 3 parallels the end of scene 2. Here the audience witnesses Romeo's grief, as a contrast to Juliet's grief in the previous scene. In scene 2, Juliet explicitly attempts to control her emotions: 'Back foolish tears', while in scene 3, Romeo's grief is melodramatic. He literally throws himself to the floor, refusing to get up, prompting Friar Lawrence to describe him as 'There on the ground, with his own tears made drunk.' The contrast between Romeo and Juliet is stark. Despite her age, Juliet is presented as far more mature than Romeo.

Shakespeare makes the parallel between scene 2 and scene 3 explicit through the repetition of the 'mansion' conceit. In scene 2, Juliet metaphorically refers to Romeo as a 'mansion'. She has 'bought' it, in terms of having married Romeo, but because the wedding has not yet been consummated, she has not 'possess'd' the mansion. The conceit conveys her anticipation of sex, a completing of the union between her and Romeo. However, in scene 3, Romeo uses the conceit of the mansion negatively. It is a 'hateful mansion' because it is the place in which his name lives. He wishes to 'sack' or destroy the mansion, for he believes it to be the source of Juliet's pain. The juxtaposition of these opposing attitudes towards the image of the 'mansion' perhaps represents the incompatibility of Romeo and Juliet, making their love even more tragic.

Romeo distances himself from his identity as a Montague, by considering it a separate entity that could exist in a part of his body. The name is personified here as lodging in the mansion of his body in the same way that he refers to the 'name's cursed hand' that murdered Tybalt. The contrast with Juliet is extended here through a comparison with Act 2, scene 2, in which Juliet recognises that a name is not 'any other part / Belonging to a man.'

The melodramatic behaviour of Romeo is evident in him taking up a dagger, as if to cut the name from his body. He has to be prevented from taking his own life as a result of the self-loathing shown by referring to himself as 'vile'. This provides another potential parallel with Juliet when, in Act 3, scene 2, she addresses the cords that Romeo told the Nurse to bring. These ropes were intended for Romeo to use to climb to Juliet's room yet here, in rhetorical apostrophe, Juliet tells the cords to come to her because 'death, not Romeo, take my maidenhead!' The implication is that she is threatening to hang herself in her grief. It may be this that prompts the Nurse to bring Romeo to Juliet.

Key Characters

Juliet

Romeo

Key Themes

Death

Love

Excess

Quotation 21

Act 3, Scene 5

Capulet:

"Out, you green-sickness carrion! Out, you baggage! / You tallow-face!"

Analysis

In Act 3, scene 4, Lord Capulet agrees to Juliet marrying Paris in three days' time. This is in stark contrast to Capulet's words in Act 1, scene 2, when he tells Paris that Juliet is too young to marry and that he should wait two more years. He also claims in Act 1, scene 2 that 'My will to her consent is but a part,' yet by Act 3 he offers her hand in marriage without seeking Juliet's consent: 'I will make a desperate tender of my child's love.'

It is Lord Capulet, rather than Juliet, who has changed his mind and the force of his anger may be a result of his damaged pride. Again, in Act 3, scene 4, he states 'I think she will be rul'd in all respects by me; nay more, I doubt it not.' Juliet's refusal to marry risks exposing Lord Capulet's hubris. It is the same kind of anger that he directs at Tybalt in Act 1, scene 5 when Tybalt questions Lord Capulet's instruction and is rebuked with 'Am I the master here, or you?'

The anaphora* of the imperative 'Out' serves to convey the extent of Lord Capulet's anger as he repeats his commands. The command is implicit in the third sentence, his anger having corrupted the structure of his sentences as well as the meter of his speech.

'Green-sickness' refers to a kind of anaemia that was believed to affect unmarried women. A clear symptom was a pale complexion, hence the chremamorphic description of Juliet as 'tallow-face' (her face being as white as a candle). This is reinforced by the metaphor 'carrion' as the pale flesh of a dead body may be alluded to, as well as the idea of Juliet being dead to him emotionally now that she has questioned his authority. Lord Capulet seems to be using this imagery to suggest that it is Juliet's unmarried status that is her weakness. This produces dramatic irony given that the audience know that Juliet is married to Romeo and reinforces the sense of Lord Capulet's ignorance.

'Baggage' gives a sense of Juliet being a burden because of rejecting the proposal; an Elizabethan audience would also recognise 'baggage' as a slang term for a prostitute so her father appears to be condemning her with the worst insults that he can think of since she has rejected a marriage that would improve the status of the family and she has failed to acknowledge the status of her father.

Key Characters

Capulet

Juliet

Key Themes

Conflict

Family

Quotation 22

Act 3, Scene 5

Nurse:

"Romeo's a dishclout to him. An eagle, madam,
Hath not so green, so quick, so fair an eye
As Paris hath."

Analysis

Despite the Nurse being portrayed as fulfilling the maternal role that Lady Capulet dismally fails in, this point in the play marks a turning-point in the relationship between the Nurse and Juliet. The Nurse does not understand the depth of the relationship between Juliet and Romeo. The bawdy language employed by her earlier in the play suggests that she focuses on the physical aspect of a relationship, something that is transitory and superficial but here she reveals to Juliet that her advice and commitment is similarly superficial.

While the Nurse supports Juliet by defending her against Capulet's treatment in this scene, it is the Nurse's failure to defend Romeo that creates a rift. Her practicality overwhelms morality. In Act 2, scene 5, the Nurse praised Romeo with superlatives. He was described as having a face 'better than any man's' and a body 'beyond compare' yet now he is a 'dishclout' in comparison to Paris. To describe someone as a 'dishclout' (dishcloth) was a proverbial Elizabethan insult; it has connotations of dirt, cheapness and disposability; the Nurse treats Romeo according to this final connotation. She immediately praises Paris through a comparison to the eyes of an eagle. She misses the point that Juliet is not interested in a comparison of the physical merits of Romeo and Paris. Despite this, the Nurse desperately stresses Paris' merits through an overwhelming asyndetic series of clauses dominated by the intensifier 'so' that attempts to convey the overwhelmingly positive qualities of Paris.

The Nurse's lack of morality is evident in her promotion of Paris when she has praised Romeo 'so many thousand times' and when she promotes a 'second match' when she knows that Juliet is already married. This causes Juliet to say of the Nurse, in soliloquy, 'Thou and my bosom henceforth shall be twain.' She will no longer confide in the Nurse and the loss of support for the young girl is almost complete; she is alienated from her father, mother, husband and now Nurse.

Key Characters	**Key Themes**
Nurse	Family
Paris	Love

Quotation 23

Act 5, Scene 1

Romeo:

"Then I defy you stars!"

Analysis

Romeo's use of rhetorical apostrophe, addressing the stars, allows Shakespeare to powerfully express Romeo's inner turmoil. The exclamation of anger and grief after receiving the false news of Juliet's death, is directed at the stars, as symbols of Fate. The audience should be reminded of the Chorus' 'star-crossed lovers' and the futility of Romeo's attempt to fight against Fate. In addition, Juliet's desire to 'cut him out into little stars' identifies Romeo with stars and may suggest to the audience that Romeo's exclamation acts as a form of self-denial; his actions are an act of defiance against himself, something that Shakespeare ironically conveys through Romeo's actions, leading to his own death and Juliet's suicide. The death of Juliet may also be foreshadowed by Romeo's defiance of the stars, since Romeo physically identifies Juliet with the stars in Act 2, scene 2, when he romantically imagines Juliet's eyes replacing the stars 'to twinkle in their spheres.'

The reference also recalls Act 1, scene 3: 'some consequence yet hanging in the stars' and Act 3, scene 1: 'O, I am fortune's fool'. While, earlier in the play, Romeo accepted being subject to Fate, his anger now fuels immediate action. To 'defy' fate suggests that Romeo is empowering himself to fight against the power of Fate. Quartos 1 to 4, published between 1597 and 1622, all use the verb 'defie', but some modern versions of the play use 'deny' following its inclusion in the fifth quarto of 1637. While the meanings are similar, 'deny' carries connotations of refusing to accept the truth, making Romeo potentially seem more passive.

Romeo's response to Balthasar's news is immediate, mirroring his impulsive response to the death of Mercutio as well as his impulsive marriage proposal. It may be this impetuosity that dooms the lovers; they are subject to Fate because they do not exercise reason or restraint.

Key Characters

Juliet

Romeo

Key Themes

Conflict

Fate

Quotation 24

Act 5, Scene 3

Romeo:

"Thou detestable maw, thou womb of death,
Gorg'd with the dearest morsel of the earth."

Analysis

The final scene begins with frenetic activity, concealment and confusion all of which contribute to the heightened emotions of both the characters and the audience. Within the first 50 lines, under cover of darkness, Paris lays flowers on Juliet's grave while sending a page to keep watch; the page alerts Paris to the arrival of Romeo and Balthasar, forcing Paris to hide; Romeo threatens Balthasar, sending him away, although Balthasar stays and when Romeo begins to break open the tomb, Paris confronts him. Shakespeare has created profound tension.

Romeo's words, addressed to the tomb through rhetorical apostrophe, complement these heightened emotions. The tomb is described through horrific imagery, conflating two body-parts: the maw (mouth) and the womb. 'Maw' is only usually used within the context of a gluttonous person, (or, more frequently, animal) and introduces the conceit of the tomb having devoured the life of Juliet in an unnecessary and offensive manner. The sense of gluttony is complemented by the use of the verb 'gorg'd' (eating to excess) and the excessive consonance of hard 'd' sounds that dominate the sentence.

Combining 'maw' and 'womb' rather than maintaining the logical consistency of the conceit with 'stomach', makes the imagery even more shocking. The oxymoronic quality of 'womb of death' reinforces this sense of wrongness, conjoining life and death in the same way that Romeo intends to add his life to this place of death. Juliet is described as the 'daintiest morsel' consumed by the tomb. She is differentiated from others on the basis of her physical attractiveness rather than any spiritual quality and Romeo later states that he intends to add his body to the tomb, not so that their souls can be joined but, in a sense that suggests physical jealousy, to stop death taking her as his 'paramour' (lover).

Juliet is referred to as 'of the earth', a phrase that works as a pun suggesting both that Juliet is the most desirable thing on earth and that she is now 'of the earth' (dead and interred beneath the ground).

Key Characters

Juliet
Romeo

Key Themes

Conflict
Death
Fate
Love

Quotation 25

Act 5, Scene 3

Romeo:

"...shake the yoke of inauspicious stars
From this world-wearied flesh."

Analysis

As Romeo prepares to drink poison, he reflects on the effect of his actions. 'Inauspicious' means ill-fated and, once again, Romeo's focus is on the stars that symbolise Fate within the play. Romeo identifies the Fate that dominates his life as one associated with bad luck.

A 'yoke' is used to fasten animals (usually oxen or horses) to a plough or cart that they must pull. The noun has connotations of being restrained and burdened, as Romeo believes himself to be by Fate. Animals could sometimes free themselves from the shackles of a yoke by shaking it. The only way in which Romeo believes himself able to free himself from this 'yoke' and defy the stars that drive the course of his life, is by metaphorically shaking himself free from the bonds of life, killing himself so that the stars no longer have power over him. His determination in Act 5, scene 1 to 'defy you, stars,' is put into effect here as he believes himself to be acting against Fate. Ironically, and tragically, he is actually fulfilling Fate, ensuring the death of himself and Juliet and ensuring that 'A pair of star-cross'd lovers take their life'.

'World-wearied' suggests that Romeo is tired by the world. The world and Fate have acted upon him, reducing him to this terrible state of mental exhaustion. It is not that he is 'world-weary', a more common phrase that would suggest that he is tired of the world, or disinterested. The use of 'flesh' rather than 'body' represents the way in which Romeo is already distancing himself from his body, something that he maintains in the following lines through rhetorical apostrophe, addressing different parts of his body as they perform their final function, a function that connects them to Juliet.

Key Characters

Romeo

Key Themes

Death

Fate

Glossary of Key Terms

Allegorical: A text in which the characters or events represent particular ideas or morals.

Allusion: An indirect reference to an idea, person or text.

Ambiguous: Having more than one meaning.

Anaphora: In rhetoric, the repetition of a word or phrase at the beginning of successive clauses.

Antithetical parallelism: Grammatical balance, where the structure of a phrase or sentence is mirrored by a similar structure but using opposite terms.

Apostrophe: In rhetoric, the process of addressing an absent or inanimate object.

Archaic: Old-fashioned.

Aside: Speech delivered by a character to the audience, as if they are thinking aloud, that is unheard by other characters on stage.

Asyndetic: A list in which none of the clauses are separated by conjunctions.

Blank verse: Unrhymed iambic pentameter.

Chorus: In Classical Greek drama, a number of actors who comment on the action of the play without participating in it.

Chremamorphism: Figurative device that refers to something animate as inanimate.

Conceit: A figure of speech which usually consists of an unexpected metaphorical comparison that is extended through multiple descriptions.

Connotation: An association inspired by word choice.

Conventions: The way that something is usually done or the rules that govern it.

Couplet: A pair of lines of poetry usually linked by rhyme.

Cratylic naming: A name that conveys a characteristic of the person named.

Denotation: Literal meaning of the thing that a word refers to.

Diminutive: A word, or form of a word, that suggests that something is small.

Dramatic irony: When the audience understands something that the character on stage does not.

Ellipsis: Omission of a word in a sentence.

Etymological: Referring to the origin and development of word meaning.

Euphemism: A word or phrase used to make a concept more polite or socially acceptable.

Exclamatory sentence: A statement that conveys excitement or strong emotion, indicated by an exclamation mark.

Existential: Relating to the nature of existence.

Fatalistic: Having the belief that all events are predetermined.

First Folio: The first collected edition of 36 of Shakespeare's plays, produced in 1623.

Foreshadowing: Providing an indication of an event that will occur later in the literary work.

Homographic pun: Two words that have the same spelling but have a different meaning.

Hyperbolic: Exaggeration.

Iambic: Adjective used to describe a unit of syllables consisting of an unstressed followed by a stressed syllable.

Idiom: An expression or saying whose meaning is not based on the literal meaning of its constituent words e.g. *kick the bucket* means die.

Imperative: Verb used to give a command.

Intensifier: An adverb used to provide emphasis.

Juxtaposition: Two things being placed together, usually to create a contrasting effect.

Macrocosmic: On the scale of the wider world or universe.

Metaphor: A figurative device in which a word is stated to be something which it is not in order to provide an implicit comparison based on characteristics.

Meter: The rhythmic patterns of stressed and unstressed syllables in a line of poetry.

Motif: Repeated idea or symbol often used to develop a theme.

Oxymoronic: The linking of two apparently contradictory terms.

Parallelism: Where the structure of a phrase or sentence is mirrored by a similar structure.

Parody: Imitation or exaggeration, often for comic effect in order to mock a subject.

Pentameter: A line of verse consisting of five metrical patterns (feet) e.g. five iambs.

Personification: Attributing human qualities to an animal or inanimate object.

Petrarchan: Adjective relating to the Italian poet Petrarch. Petrarch devised the sonnet form consisting of two stanzas often focusing on the suffering of a melodramatic lover.

Phonological: Relating to the pattern of sounds.

Quarto: A small book constructed from single printed pieces of paper folded into four leaves (8 pages). This made them cheap editions.

Quatrain: A four-line stanza, often with an alternating rhyme scheme.

Semantic field: A set of words linked by related meanings.

Sibilant: A hissing sound created by 's' or 'c'.

Simile: A figure of speech in which an explicit comparison is made between two things.

Soliloquy: A speech delivered by a character who is alone on stage, revealing their thoughts to the audience.

Sonnet: A form of poetry consisting of 14 lines. The English sonnet usually includes three quatrains and a couplet with an **abab cdcd efef gg** rhyme scheme.

Stichomythia: Short exchanges of dialogue in a drama.

Synonym: A word that has the same or very similar meaning.

Tripartite: Consisting of three parts.

About the author of this guide

Mark Birch has been a teacher of English for 25 years and the Head of the English Faculty in six schools; he is currently Head of English at Hull Collegiate School. Having achieved his degree at King's College Cambridge, Mark went on to study a PGCE in English at Sheffield University. Mark has been judged as outstanding in every observation of his teaching career and his passion for literary analysis has informed the criticism to be found in this guide. As well as teaching and writing, Mark enjoys producing revision videos that can be found on his YouTube channel.

About the editor of this guide

Hannah Rabey is Head of English at a school in Oxfordshire. Hannah studied Literature and History at the University of East Anglia before studying for her PGCE at the University of Oxford. Hannah is a GCSE examiner and is experienced with teaching all of the texts in the 25 Key Quotations revision guide series.

Printed in Great Britain
by Amazon

20958753R00041